Created by Tara Boykin

Beginner Piano Book

INDEX

Hot Cross Buns

E D C

E D C

C C C C

D D D D

E D C

Mary Had a Little Lamb

E D C D E E E

D D D E G G

E D C D E E E E

D D E D C

Twinkle Twinkle Little Star

C C ↑G G A A G

F F E E D D C

↑G G F F E E D

↑G G F F E E D

C C ↑G G A A G

F F E E D D C

C CD C ↑F E

C CD C ↑G F

C C ↑C A F E D

↑B♭ B♭ A F G F

Au Clair de la Lune

C C C D E D

C E D D C :||

D D D D ↓A A

↑D C B A G

↑C C C D E D

C E D D C

Row Row Row Your Boat

C C C DE

E DE FG

↑CCC ↓GGG

EEE CCC

↑G FE DC

Skip To My Lou

E C E EE G

↓D B D DD F

E C E EE G

↓D EFE D C C

Yankee Doodle

C C D E C E D

C C D E C B

C C D E F E D C

B G A B C C

London Bridge

G A G F E F G

↓D E F E F G

G A G F E F G

↓D ↑G E C

Ring Around the Rosie

G GE ↑AG E F

G GE ↑AG E

G E G E

EG G ↓C

Frère Jacques

C D E C   C D E C

E F G   E F G

G A G F E   C

G A G F E   C

C ↓G ↑C   C ↓G ↑C

This Old Man

G E G G E G

A G F E D E F

E F G ↓C C C C

C D E F G

G ↓D D F E D C

I'm a Little Teapot

C DE FG ↑C

A C ↓G

F F FE E

D D DC

C DE FG ↑C

A C ↓G

↑C AG GF E D C

Hush Little Baby

(↓)G ↑E E E F

E D D D

↓G G ↑D D D

D E D C C

↓G ↑E E F E D D

↓G G ↑D D D

D E D C C

Bingo

(↓)G ↑C C C ↓G A A G

G ↑C C D D E C

E E F F F

D D E E E

C C D D D

C B G A B C C

Pop Goes the Weasel

(↓)G ↑C C D D E

G E C

↓G ↑C C D D E C

↓G ↑C C D D E

G E C

↑A ↓D F E C

You Are My Sunshine

(↓)G ↑C D E E

E D E C C

C D E F A

A G F E

C D E F A

A G F E C

C D E F D D E C

The Wheels on the Bus

(↓)G ↑C C C C E

G E C

D B G

↑G E C

↓G ↑C C C C E

G E C

D ↓G G ↑C

Baa Baa Black Sheep

G G ↑D D EEEE D

C C B B A A G

↑D DD C C B BB A

↑D DD CCCC

B BB A

G G ↑D D EEEE D

C C B B A A G

Old MacDonald

G G G ↓D E E D

↑B B A A G 

↓D D G G G **x2**

G G G G G G

G G G G G G

G G G ↓D E E D

↑B B A A G

Ode To Joy

E E F G G F E D

C C D E E D D

E E F G G F E D

C C D E D C C

D D E C D EFE C

D EFE D C D ↓G

↑E E F G G F E D

C C D E D C C

The Itsy Bitsy Spider

(↓)G ↑C C C D E E

E D C D E C

E E F G G

F E F G E

C C D E E

D C D E C ↓G

G ↑C C C D E E

E D C D E C

Three Blind Mice

E D C   E D C

↑G F F E   G F F E

G ↑C   C B A B C   ↓G G

G ↑C C C B A B C   ↓G G

G G ↑C C B A B C ↓G G G

G   E   D   C

Rockabye Baby

(↓)B D ↑B A G

↓B D ↑G F♯

↓C D ↑C B

A A G E D

B D ↑B A G

↓B D ↑G F♯

E D ↑G ↑C B G

A ↓E F♯ G

She'll Be Coming Around the Mountain

D E G G G G

E D B D ↑G

G A B B B B

↑D B A G A

↑D C B B B B A G

G G E E E E ↑A G

F♯ E D D D D

↑B A ↓E F♯ G

If You're Happy and You Know It

(↓)G G ↑C C C C C C

B C D (clap, clap!)

↓G G ↑D D D D D D

C D E (clap, clap!)

E E F F F F ↓A A

↑F F E E E D C C

E E D D D C B B

A B C (clap, clap!)

The Ants Go Marching In

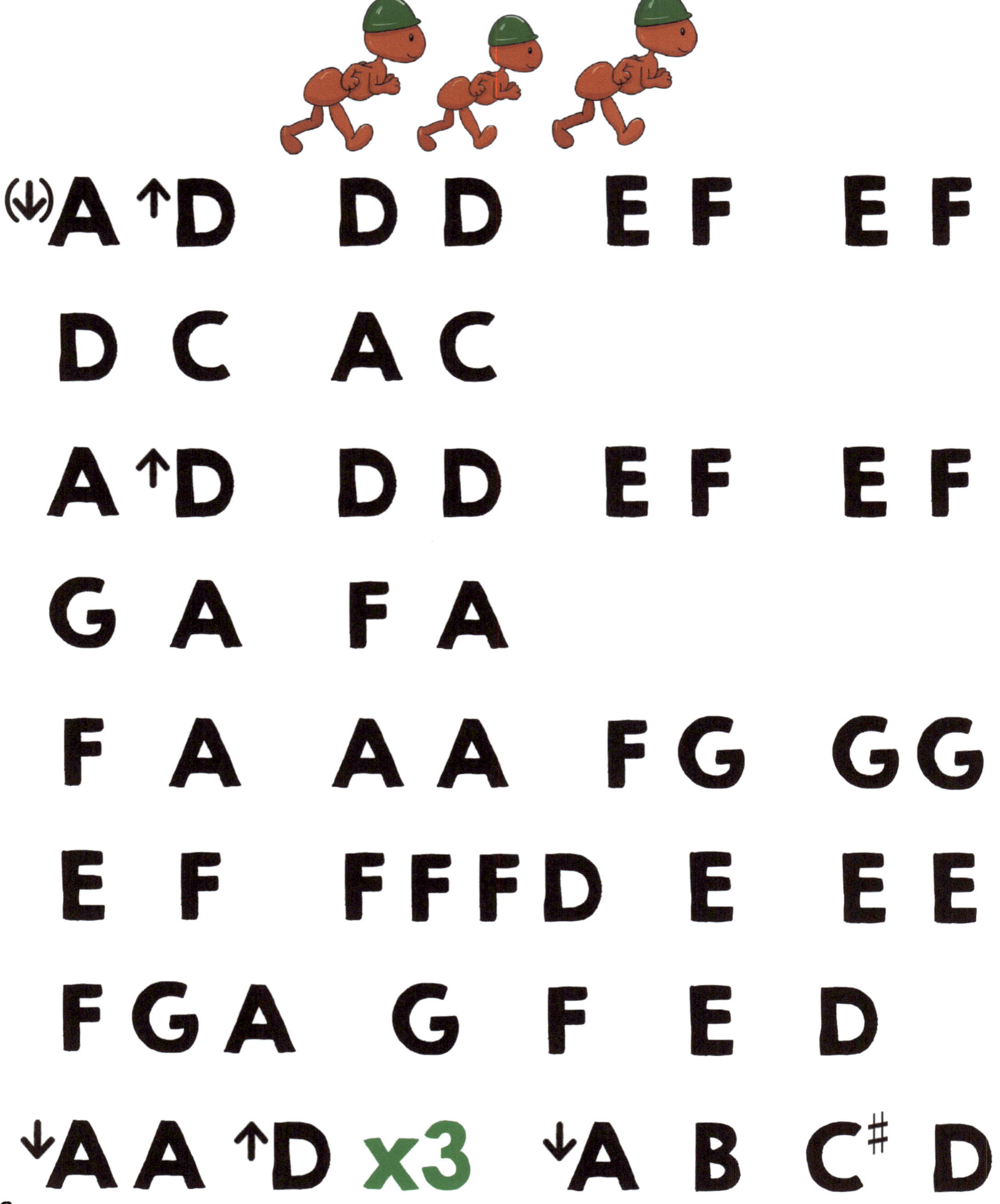

Cascade Method Certificate

Congratulations to

____

for finishing the Beginner Piano Book!!!

Teacher: ______________________________ **Date:** ______________

www.ingramcontent.com/pod-product-compliance
Ingram Content Group UK Ltd.
Pitfield, Milton Keynes, MK11 3LW, UK
UKHW060122300726
14090UKWH00002B/312

* 9 7 9 8 6 1 3 5 7 6 5 0 0 *